Original title:
Beneath the Branches

Copyright © 2025 Creative Arts Management OÜ
All rights reserved.

Author: Gideon Shaw
ISBN HARDBACK: 978-1-80567-362-0
ISBN PAPERBACK: 978-1-80567-661-4

Veiled Moments in the Woods

Squirrels in tuxedos chase after a breeze,
While owls play poker beneath sky-high trees.
The mushrooms are dancing, a whimsical sight,
Their polka dot caps swirl in the dimmed twilight.

The raccoon, a chef, stirs his wild stew,
Adding acorns and nuts, just for the crew.
With laughter that echoes, the shadows grow long,
As critters join in for a woodland song.

Enigma of the Overhanging Leaves

Lizards in sunglasses lounge on a line,
Arguing if sunbathing is truly divine.
A snail with a top hat takes his sweet time,
Claiming that fashion is hardly a crime.

Bumblebees buzz in a comedic ballet,
While ants do a conga, hip-hip-hooray!
The wind whispers secrets with giggles and glee,
In this leafy retreat where all want to be.

Harmony of Hidden Heights

Chirping crickets compose a tune,
Under moon's glow, they boogie till noon.
A fox with a flute plays a jazzy refrain,
As fireflies twinkle, embracing the gain.

Raccoons are frolicking, stealing the show,
Dressed up as bandits, they navigate slow.
A whoopee cushion plays a prank on the owl,
There's laughter and joy, oh what a howl!

The Treetop Reverie

High above, a sloth hangs with style and flair,
In the midst of his nap, with not a care.
A parrot quips jokes, colors vibrant and loud,
Testing the laughter of the leafy crowd.

A bear on a tightrope, balancing divine,
With a tutu of flowers, he's looking just fine.
Tree branches sway gently in rhythm and rhyme,
As nature's own circus performs every time.

Hushed Conversations of the Woods

The squirrels plan their heist tonight,
With acorns tossed in a grand old fight.
While owls pretend to be wise and sage,
Bickering raccoons steal the stage.

A rabbit joins in with a cheeky grin,
"Who knows what trouble we'll get in?"
With every rustle, laughter spreads,
As whispers float above their heads.

Reflections in the Underbrush

Frogs in tuxedos on lily pads,
Croaking secrets, not feeling bad.
The crickets hold a concert show,
While fireflies dance with a flashy glow.

Beneath the ferns, a hedgehog dreams,
Of cheese and pies and endless beams.
Each creature giggles in the light,
Sharing tales until the night.

The Secret Language of Trees

The oak is wise, the birch a tease,
"Let's prank the flowers!" it gently wheezes.
The willow whispers by the stream,
"Did you hear about the squirrel's scheme?"

As branches sway in gleeful chat,
"I think that bug is wearing a hat!"
The winds carry their rumors high,
As birds giggle and flutter by.

In the Soft Glow of the Twilight Glade

The bunnies bounce in a playful race,
Chasing shadows in a merry chase.
A raccoon juggles with three shiny stones,
While owls chuckle in low, gruff tones.

The mist begins to tickle the trees,
"Time for a bath!" says a bee with ease.
In the glow, they all take a seat,
Sharing stories, oh what a treat!

Musings of the Leafed Sanctuary

A squirrel debates with a wise old crow,
Who steals the acorns? They both claim to know.
The sun flickers through leaf and branch,
While the ants throw a party—oh, what a chance!

A rabbit bets on a turtle's great race,
But the turtle just smiles, with grace on his face.
The flowers gossip, they twist and they sway,
As the bees hum along, making music all day.

Solace Within the Shade

A grasshopper wearing a top hat so fine,
Judges the dance-offs, while sipping on wine.
The daisies wear laughter, their petals aglow,
As the wind tells a joke, and the branches all bow.

A raccoon brings snacks, he's clever and sly,
While the fox sets the stage for a grand puppet fly.
With giggles and wiggles, the critters unite,
In this shady fun zone, everything feels right.

The Enchanted Arboretum

A chattering chipmunk, a feast he has found,
And the owls are nodding, they're wise and they're profound.
The swing of a branch is an air-swinging show,
As the beetles breakdance, putting on a glow.

The sun shines like glitter, the leaves start to giggle,
A butterfly slips and begins to wiggle.
As the breeze plays the ukulele so sweet,
Nature's own cabaret—can't be beat!

Beneath the Skyline of Leaves

A snail in a shell has a gossiping spree,
Telling tales of the wind and the buzzing bee.
With each windblown story, the branches all sway,
As the sun starts to dip, making shadows at play.

The flowers compete in a beauty grand race,
While a lizard cracks jokes with a grin on his face.
In this leafy arena, where laughter runs free,
Every day is a joke, come roll with me!

Embraced by Nature's Ornament

In the shade of leafy cheer,
Squirrels dance without a fear,
Wiggly worms in line for lunch,
Nearby, a goat is on a hunch.

A bird with socks upon its feet,
Takes a look, and thinks it's neat,
While bunnies hop with cotton tails,
Creating mischief without fails.

The flowers giggle in the breeze,
As bees wear hats, oh what a tease,
A charm all wrapped in nature's glow,
Where laughter blooms, and joy will flow.

The Stillness of the Grove

A turtle did a ballet twirl,
Stuck in mud, it gave a whirl,
While crickets chirped a silly tune,
And danced around a plastic spoon.

An owl with glasses reads the news,
Reporting what no one can use,
He takes a sip from a twigged cup,
And says, 'I think it's time to sup!'

A deer plays hide-and-seek from trees,
While chipmunks caterwaul with ease,
In stillness, joy and chaos blend,
Each leaf an unexpected friend.

Tales Told in Timber

Once a branch had a good chat,
With ants who claimed they found a hat,
Together, they shared a silly tale,
Of a mushroom that rode a snail.

A woodpecker writes novels there,
Describing life without a care,
It taps away with constant glee,
While frogs croak out their poetry.

With a twist of bark and a laugh,
The tales of trees begin to craft,
Beneath the laughter of the leaves,
Nature's stories turn to thieves.

Gestures of the Garden's Heart

A gnome attempts to grow a beard,
While sunflowers laugh, feeling cheered,
They tickle bees as they go by,
In silly antics, none are shy.

A rabbit wears a tiny crown,
While daisies giggle, floppy brown,
They cheer him on, a royal feast,
Creating chaos — what a beast!

In pots of soil, the roots converse,
Recounting things in verse and verse,
The garden blooms with joy and fray,
Nature's funny, bright ballet.

Reverent Hush of Nature

In the woods where squirrels plot,
They giggle and laugh at thoughts they've got.
A bird on a branch sings a silly tune,
While rabbits jump high, dancing to the moon.

Under leaves where shadows play,
Ants march in lines, like kids at a ballet.
Bees buzz by with a comedic flair,
As frogs in a chorus croak without a care.

Glimmers in the Brown and Green

The sun peeks through leaves with a cheeky grin,
Tickling the flowers, letting the fun begin.
A snail slides down with a glamorous flair,
While worms do the cha-cha, unaware of their hair.

The tiny critters hold a grand affair,
With dandelions as hats, oh what a bear!
An acorn rolls in, brings laughter galore,
As nature herself cannot help but snore.

The Life Below the Boughs

There's a mouse who's lost in a tall grassy maze,
While a chubby raccoon stumbles in a haze.
The laughter of owls echo in the night,
As fireflies dance, exchanging delight.

A hedgehog slips, doubles over a twig,
The chorus of nature is quite the gig.
Beneath the great and glorious arch,
Every critter joins in their hilarious march.

The Forest's Whispering Art

Deep in the woods, a tree starts to plot,
With vines in a twist, it forgets what it's got.
The laughter of leaves sways with the breeze,
Tickled by whispers of silly little pleas.

A bear tells a joke, and birds fall from flight,
While butterflies flutter in glee at the sight.
The brook bubbles over with giggles so sweet,
In the midst of the chaos, all critters compete.

The Language of the Leaves

Whispers of green chatter away,
As squirrels play tag in bright display.
Leaves gossip low, a rustling spree,
While acorns debate who's best on a tree.

A wind tickles, causing a laugh,
Branches shake, like a silly giraffe.
Nature's jest, pure comedy relief,
While critters dance without any grief.

Sunshine streams through laughter's glow,
Each leaf a comedian, putting on a show.
With puns in rustles, the forest ignites,
Tickles and giggles are nature's delights.

In this leafy theater, all are invited,
As frolicsome fauna leaves none divided.
For under this canopy, joy takes its flight,
Turning moments of silence into sheer delight.

Secrets in the Skeletal Branches

The branches twist like a grand old story,
With vines that wriggle in joyful glory.
Old bark creaks, making jokes about age,
While pinecones laugh, center stage.

Beneath a moon that can't stop grinning,
Crickets chirp, like they're all winning.
A branch might tickle a passerby,
As shadows dance, oh my, oh my!

Leaves pretend to be shy little sprites,
While squirrels hold court on fanciful heights.
With every rustle, a secret is spun,
Amongst the branches, the laughter is fun.

Elders chuckle from their roost high above,
Bestowing wisdom wrapped up in love.
With every chirp and every crack,
Nature's shadows all share a laugh on the track.

In the Presence of Ancients

Tall trees stand like grumpy old men,
Sharing tall tales again and again.
Roots grumble jokes about their long life,
As the wind joins in, adding to strife.

Leaves flap like they're waving hello,
While families of owls put on a show.
With each hoot, they mock ages past,
Reminding the beetles: "Your days won't last!"

Twists and turns in bark hold secrets so deep,
As saplings giggle, trying not to leap.
The wise oaks chuckle, "We've seen much fun,
Remember, dear sprout, this is just one run!"

In shadows where sunlight rarely intrudes,
Laughter resounds amidst solemn moods.
For even the oldest know life's little game,
And the forest's laughter will always remain.

A Bough of Secret Dreams

On a bough where the dreams take flight,
Squirrels debate the best way to write.
With acorns as pens, they craft a new tale,
While jays share jokes in a riotous gale.

Fluttering leaves wear hats made of glee,
Pretending they're wise 'neath the old maple tree.
Crickets, like jesters, perform in a ring,
As evening descends, inviting them to sing.

A raccoon winks, "Hey, want a sneak peek?
At the critter council where we all speak!"
Gossamer dreams drift on each gentle breeze,
Tickling the branches, aiming to please.

And when starlight sparkles, the branches conspire,
To turn every hush into something desired.
For laughter and whimsy are hidden in seams,
Where the forest thrives on a bough of dreams.

Beneath the Green Enchantment

In a land where owls wear their specs,
And squirrels claim they run the tech,
The flowers giggle, whispering tales,
Of mischief played on wandering snails.

A frog in a top hat takes a leap,
While grassy beds watch all this creep,
The trees chuckle, shake their green heads,
As rabbits dance on their tiny beds.

Lullabies of the Leafy Realm

A moth in a cape sings soft and sweet,
While chairs made of leaves hold grand banquets to eat,
The fireflies blink in a quirky rhyme,
As shadows play tricks, lost in their prime.

A raccoon in pajamas sneaks by with a grin,
Collecting old treasures from where he's been,
The dandelions toast with a soft, fluffy cheer,
To the sound of leaf laughter that floats in the air.

Reverie in the Wooded Silence

In the hush where soft breezes play,
A gopher holds court at the end of the day,
He tells tales of finding a lost pair of shoes,
While curious mice sip on dew from their views.

The rabbits roll dice by the old willow's shade,
As a turtle in sneakers deals out the trade,
The pines hum a tune, in a bright, lively scent,
While everything laughs at the time that they spent.

A Dance of Sunlight and Shade

Under rays that sprinkle and tease,
The ants cheer on a parade of bees,
With confetti of petals in the soft breeze,
While chipmunks juggle acorns with ease.

A cicada croons in the carefree light,
About a squirrel who dreams of taking flight,
The shadows spin tales of the day's silly glee,
As vines wrap around in a happy marquee.

The Songs of Dappled Sun

In the green where shadows play,
Squirrels dance in a wild ballet.
Chasing tails, they leap and spin,
While the birds laugh; let the games begin!

A cheeky crow caws way too loud,
Interrupting the gossip of a proud cloud.
The flowers giggle in a breeze,
A party starting, come if you please!

Acorns roll like tiny balls,
Dodging feet on the forest halls.
The sun peeks through, a playful tease,
While rabbits hop with the greatest of ease!

So gather round with snacks to share,
In this funny world, beyond compare.
Laughter mingles with the rustling leaves,
As nature weaves tales in funny weaves!

In the Heart of the Arboreal

In the heart where the sunbeams burst,
A chipmunk's joke is always first.
With a nutty grin, he cracks the wise,
While the wise old owl just rolls his eyes.

The vines twist in a hilarious dance,
As bees buzz in a silly romance.
They bump and tumble, creating a scene,
Nature's circus, bright and serene!

Mice in tuxedos tip their hats,
While the turtles race, but they just chat.
The flowers debate who wore it best,
While ladybugs join in on the jest!

The wind carries tales of each funny plight,
As shadows stretch and the stars invite.
Join the revelry with nature's jest,
In this goofy, green, arboreal quest!

Chronicles of the Sylvan Realm

In the realm where mischief reigns,
A raccoon plots amidst the gains.
With a mask and paws in the pantry,
He flips a lid; oh, what a shanty!

Dancing leaves, they start to clap,
As the hedgehogs swap their cozy nap.
A frog in a top hat takes a leap,
In the chronicles where giggles creep!

The trees toss shade like silly hats,
To hide the laughter from the spats.
The squirrels argue, who can crack,
A joke so funny, they'll never look back!

So grab a twig and make a sign,
Join the tales of the sylvan line.
Adventure awaits in each funny plot,
In this forest of laughter, tied in a knot!

The Quietude of the Verdant Den

In a cozy nook where laughter streams,
A wise old toad stirs up the dreams.
He tells of mishaps from days of yore,
While the crickets play their music core.

The trees lean in to catch each word,
As the ants form lines, excitement stirred.
A game of tag, oh, what a sight,
In the quietude, all is light!

The ferns giggle with each little tale,
While a rabbit hops and leaves a trail.
His ears flop like magic wands,
In this den where joy responds!

So settle down on the soft, green floor,
With secrets, laughs, and tales galore.
In nature's lap, time can bend,
Finding humor in the verdant den!

In the Shade of Evergreen Dreams

In the forest, squirrels play,
Chasing acorns every day.
A wise old owl with a grin,
Says, "Life's a nut, so dive right in!"

Rabbits hop with plenty of flair,
Tickled by the fragrant air.
While bees buzz in a dance so sweet,
Joining in with happy feet.

A raccoon's hat, oh what a sight!
He wears it proudly, day and night.
A chipmunk sings a jolly tune,
Picturing a dance with the moon.

From leafy chairs, we laugh and cheer,
Telling tales of joy and cheer.
In this shade, all worries cease,
Nature's fun, a gift of peace.

The Tapestry of Tree Shadows

Under the trees, what a sight,
A shadow puppet show tonight.
Where squirrels act with flair and grace,
And we all laugh, our worries chase.

A bear rolls by with a tumble and twist,
He's just looking for a fish to kiss.
While the owls hoot in nightly glee,
Wishing they could join the spree.

A raccoon joins in, does a jig,
His moves are strange, but quite big.
The trees sway as they cast their charms,
While crickets sing, raising alarms.

As shadows dance, the stars appear,
We toast to joy, and lots of cheer.
In this wild theater, no need to know,
What tale will come, or where it'll go.

Treading Through the Thicket

In a thicket, oh what a mess,
We tumble and trip, but we still confess.
A porcupine waves, saying hello,
"Watch your step, or see me go!"

With branches hanging, it's a game,
Who'll shout loudest with laughable claim?
A hedgehog rolls in a ball so tight,
"I'd join the fun, but I'm just not right!"

Through brambles thick and vines that cling,
We chase the laughter that critters bring.
A frog croaks jokes from a lily pad,
His punchlines leave us all quite glad.

Together we frolic, in this green maze,
Finding humor amidst leafy praise.
In this wild thicket, let's roam free,
For every stumble is comedy!

Serenade of Twisting Vines

Twisting vines, like knots of fun,
A lizard slips, thinking he's won.
With a flick of tail, he sways with ease,
While frogs jump high, just to tease.

A clingy vine wraps a bird so bold,
"Help! I'm stuck!" is what he told.
But swaying branches just giggle away,
As butterflies dance and brightly play.

Through leafy realms, we skip and sing,
In this dreamy place, there's no king.
The whispers of nature, a jazzy beat,
Make every step feel light and sweet.

So let's twirl 'neath these leafy hats,
With funny friends and silly chats.
In this serenade, joy takes the lead,
Nature's chuckles are all we need.

Gaze into the Shaded Abyss

In a daze, I poke my nose,
At squirrels throwing acorn foes.
A chubby chipmunk rides my shoe,
I scream, he laughs, and off he flew.

A shadow slips, it laughs, it hides,
My sandwich flies, my drink derides.
From leafy canopies above,
A bird drops snacks — oh sweet, sweet love!

The ants parade, they take their stand,
A miniature march across my hand.
With tiny hats and shiny shoes,
They mock my plight, oh, what a ruse!

Yet here I sit, in nature's play,
Among the giggles of the fray.
A tickling breeze, a ticklish jest,
In the shaded abyss, I find my rest.

Under the Boughs of Time

In shadows strong, my hair goes wild,
A chipmunk thinks I'm just a child.
He clambers up, all bold and spry,
And steals my hat; oh me, oh my!

With leafy quips from every side,
The trees all chuckle, can't abide.
They swap old tales of bugs and birds,
While I sit wondering with the nerds.

A breeze will sneak, it tugs at pants,
The forest giggles; come, take a chance!
Through knotted branches peek the skies,
As laughing clouds pull funny sighs.

What time is it under leafy cheer?
A sketchy hand, a ticklish sneer.
Here in the mess of roots and rhyme,
I dance along, ignoring time!

Life Among the Sprays

Sprays of laughter fill the air,
With bees a-buzzing everywhere.
A daisy sings a froggy song,
As I join in, but not for long.

The grass tickles my toes, oh dear!
A hedgehog rolls—a jab or cheer?
With each bounce, a giggle shows,
As nature's jokes are lined in rows.

A splash of mud, a slide or two,
The puddles form a dance anew.
With every waddle, splish, and splash,
The thirsty ferns, they watch the crash!

Yet here we roam, in frolic's spree,
With woodland critters, wild, crazy glee.
Life in green's a jest, you see,
A comic plight in symphony.

Enchanted by Woodland Shadows

In shadow's grip, the jokes unfold,
A curvy vine, nature's hold.
A lizard struts in quite a flair,
Teasing me with his reptile air.

Mushrooms giggle, they cluster tight,
Holding secrets of the night.
While owls hoot their wise refrain,
I laugh aloud, they call it plain!

The branches twist, they shake and sway,
The hidden critters join the play.
A rabbit winks, my fear deflates,
Amidst the shadows, joy awaits.

With every rustle, a joke spins round,
In this enchanted, leafy ground.
So let us skip and dance with cheer,
Amongst the shadows, laughter's near!

The Hideaway of Nature's Embrace

In a world of leafy cheer,
Squirrels dance, with nuts so near.
They chatter loud, what a sight!
Planning parties, oh what a fright!

Frogs in hats jump with glee,
Throwing parties by the tree.
Bees wear shades, sipping tea,
Nature's humor, wild and free.

Ducks in bowties waddle by,
Quacking tunes that catch the eye.
While rabbits play hopscotch in the grass,
Nature's laughter, a friendly pass.

A Canopy of Dreams

Underneath the leafy sway,
A snail sings jazz, brightens the day.
His friends, the ants, tap their feet,
A dance-off here, oh what a treat!

Twirling birds in fancy clothes,
Swinging low and striking poses.
They joke about their tiny wings,
While butterflies wear diamond rings.

A raccoon with a chef's tall hat,
Mixing acorns, oh that's where it's at!
He serves up stew with a cheeky wink,
In this haven, who'd dare to blink?

Serenity Amongst the Twigs

In a glen where wildlings roam,
A hedgehog sets up a cozy home.
With pillows made from moss and fluff,
He invites all, saying, 'Enough is enough!'

The badger brings some berry pies,
Witty jokes and some silly ties.
They laugh and play, oh what fun,
Under the warmth of the bright sun.

All gather 'round for a game of chance,
An epic showdown, a woodland dance.
With laughter ringing through the air,
In nature's heart, joy everywhere.

Starlight Filtered Through Foliage

When twilight whispers through the leaves,
A band of foxes forms a thieves.
They plot to steal the moon's bright glow,
To light their game of tag below.

Fireflies flash their fancy lights,
As crickets play on summer nights.
A wise old owl rolls his eyes,
"Quit stealing stars! That's not so wise!"

Under twinkling skies they tease,
Nature's jokes carried by the breeze.
Chasing shadows, what a sight!
In nature's laughter, pure delight.

Silhouettes of Seclusion

In shadows where the squirrels play,
Laughing at the world, come what may.
The sun peeks through with a cheeky grin,
While critters plot their mischief within.

A raccoon wears a mask, oh so sly,
Stealing snacks as he scurries by.
The breeze whispers secrets, soft and loud,
As nature chuckles, feeling proud.

A squirrel with acorns stashes away,
Counting his treasures, day by day.
The world above seems far too neat,
While below, it's a nutty retreat!

And here we sit in our leafy dome,
Sharing smiles, feeling quite at home.
Life's little quirks, we hold them dear,
In our hidden world, laughter is clear.

A Symphony of Branches

Up in the canopy, the birds will croon,
A tune so silly, it makes us swoon.
A parrot in socks struts with such flair,
As melodies twirl through the open air.

The owls hoot rhythm, a wise old beat,
While woodpeckers drum with relentless heat.
A chorus of giggles serenades the day,
Nature's orchestra in a comical way.

A baby raccoon sings a flat note,
While the mama sways, trying to gloat.
The harmony of life brings joy galore,
As branches sway, we ask for more.

Forget the silence, bring on the cheer,
For beneath the boughs, it's fun right here.
In this wild concert, we're all a part,
With laughter and nature, a work of art!

Kinship of Roots and Reality

The roots below hold stories untold,
Of mischief and whispers, bold and old.
Worms throw a party, it's quite the scene,
While ants line dance, so spry and keen.

From the mud emerges quite a sight,
A frog in a tux; isn't he bright?
He leaps with flair, then takes a bow,
Declaring, "I'm the star; don't you see how?"

Beneath the ground, the laughter roars,
As friends share tales of their hidden scores.
Roots intertwine with giggles of glee,
In this family of soil, we find unity.

So raise a toast with your leafy friends,
To the silly secrets that nature sends.
In this merry gathering, it's clear to see,
Reality's best when we're wild and free.

The Cloak of Extreme Green

Wearing a cloak of vibrant hue,
The trees hold secrets, yes it's true.
But in their branches, the laughter flows,
As nature pranks from head to toes.

A lizard in shades looks quite a sight,
Doing a dance, oh what a delight!
With each twist, he nearly slips,
While butterflies giggle, enjoying the quips.

The mossy carpet ticks and tocks,
Hiding the critters in silly frocks.
Together they thrive in playful schemes,
Chasing the sunlight and living their dreams.

So cheers to the green and all its lore,
For underneath laughter continues to soar.
In this enchanted place, we laugh and play,
Wrapped in nature's cloak, come join the ballet!

The Heartbeat of the Understory

Amid the ferns, a beat so weird,
A squirrel dances like it's cheered,
With acorns flying left and right,
Oh what a mess, what a sight!

The jays are laughing, making noise,
While ants march by like little boys,
A snail slides past with style and grace,
It gives the bramble a funny face.

The mushrooms giggle, the shadows play,
With every rustle, life's ballet,
A rabbit hops, trips on a root,
And tumbles down in a fuzzy suit.

So join the party, have some fun,
Under the greens, beneath the sun,
Embrace the chaos, let it roll,
The heartbeat here will touch your soul.

In the Arms of the Oak

What secrets hide in branches wide?
A raccoon peeks, eyes full of pride,
He wears a mask, so sly and keen,
Who knew trees had such a scene?

A woodpecker knocks like he's the boss,
While squirrels scold with a haughty gloss,
Beneath the leaves, a party's brewing,
Catch a glance, it's all worth pursuing.

A cat naps snug on a sunlit bough,
Dreaming of mice or chasing a cow,
The oak just laughs, its limbs do sway,
In the gentle breeze of a lazy day.

So raise your glass to the life we find,
In our leafy friends, we're all entwined,
With roots so deep and stories bold,
In their embrace, the laughter's told.

Reflections of the Silent Canopy

Up above, the leaves convene,
In whispers soft, they form a scene,
A bird critiques, while others jest,
Nature's theater at its best.

A frog croaks loud, thinking it's cool,
His regal stance, a froggy fool,
While crickets chirp their nightly tune,
Adding flair to the dinner soon.

A raccoon tips over trashy finds,
As laughter echoes through the pines,
With every stumble, each creature sways,
In this mischief, joy parades.

So lift your heart, let laughter flow,
Among the branches, let love grow,
For in the quiet, and in the cheer,
Life's funny moments always near.

Whispers in the Underbrush

Among the thickets, a dance is spun,
With critters clamoring, having fun,
A hedgehog rolls, thinks it's a game,
  While badgers tease, just the same.

A bunny hops, loses his hat,
While a fox observes, sneaky and fat,
They laugh and play, it's quite the spree,
  Nature's comedy, wild and free.

In shadows deep, the mischief grows,
With lilting chirps and sneaky toes,
A parade of critters, all unique,
In this green realm, the laughter's cheek.

So listen close, as tales untold,
In every rustle, watch laughter unfold,
In the underbrush, life shares its light,
With whispers of joy, both day and night.

A Haven for the Spirits of Green

In a cozy nook where squirrels conspire,
Laughter echoes like a playful choir,
Frogs wear hats and dance on logs,
While birds sip tea with chatting dogs.

The trees gossip, their branches sway,
Whispering tales of a sunny day,
Critters juggling acorns and pies,
A comedy show beneath the skies.

Mice in costumes parade with flair,
While chipmunks judge from their comfy chair,
The butterflies giggle, twirl, and glide,
In this green haven, where joys collide.

With mushroom caps as chairs in rows,
Everyone's laughing, no one knows,
That in this realm of silliness vast,
Nature's humor is unsurpassed.

The Comfortable Conglomerate of Nature

Under leafy shades, where laughter's found,
A skunk tells jokes, and the rabbits abound,
A turtle cracks puns at a snail's slow pace,
While flowers giggle, oh what a place!

The daisies gossip about dapper bees,
While frogs in tuxedos croak with ease,
A hedgehog juggles dandelion fluff,
Saying, 'Life's a circus, but never too tough!'

The clouds drift by, wearing silly grins,
As the sun tickles leaves and twirls with spins,
In this comfy haven where giggles ring,
Nature's laughter is the best kind of spring.

With daisies as cushions and acorns for snacks,
The critters lounge easy, no worry it lacks,
Here in this spot, where the funny's alive,
Every plant and beast shares a joyous high five.

Fragments of Light, Fragments of Life

Through branches we peek at the world of fun,
Dancing with shadows, we laugh and run,
A raccoon with maracas leads a parade,
While sunlight winks, in a playful charade.

Lemonade spills from a playful blue jay,
While critters play tag in a bright, sunny ray,
A rabbit in sneakers hops quick as a flame,
Chasing a turtle who's 'slow at the game!'

The goldfinch cracks jokes that make daisies sway,
While grasshoppers dance with their pesky ballet,
With fragments of joy shining bright from above,
Nature's own theatre, a laugh in each shove!

As shadows grow long, and the sun starts to yawn,
The giggles still echo, from dusk until dawn,
In this whimsical world, we come alive,
Where fragments of light help our spirits thrive.

Fragments of Light, Fragments of Life

From branches drop beams of sparkling cheer,
Where squirrels play tricks, and all creatures leer,
A butterfly dons a sparkly crown,
While ants start a conga line, whirling around.

In this patch of green, mirth surely reigns,
As the sun does its dance on the colorful plains,
With frogs pulling pranks on the unsuspecting,
Nature's comedy show is ever perfecting.

A raccoon wearing shades struts down the lane,
While a hedgehog sneezes—a ticklish refrain,
The petals of flowers burst into giggles,
As moonlight joins in with its gentle wiggles.

So under these leaves where the humor is rife,
We toast to the joy of this playful life,
In a world where laughter and light intertwine,
Fragments of fun in nature's design.

In the Embrace of Nature's Veil

The squirrel got a snack attack,
He stole a nut, then made a crack.
A bird sang loud, a wishy-wash,
While ants debated, 'Who's the boss?'

A rabbit danced, forgot to hop,
He tripped on roots, went belly flop.
The flowers giggled in the breeze,
As frogs composed their symphonies.

The sun peeked through the leaves so bright,
A chipmunk thought it was a light.
He tried to catch it, what a sight,
And stumbled back with tiny fright.

So here we play, a circus grand,
Where leaves and laughter go hand in hand.
With nature's jokes and jolly sounds,
Here joy in every corner bounds.

Hidden Pathways of the Forest

The paths were twisted, turned around,
Where every step made giggles sound.
A gnome was lost, without his map,
Reversed his hat and took a nap.

The trees were thick, the vines had fun,
They tripped a frog, a woodland run.
The toadstool chairs were full of cheer,
As mushrooms whispered, 'Sit right here!'

A porcupine wore boots too bright,
He slipped and slid, what a delight.
With every stumble, laughter grew,
The forest danced, a wacky crew.

So wander forth, through leafy maze,
Where every turn brings silly ways.
In hidden nooks, the merry cheer,
Would make your worries disappear.

The Stillness of Mossy Haven

The mossy floor, a soft embrace,
Where sleepy lizards found their space.
A turtle yawned, and slipped, oh dear,
He laughed aloud, 'I'll hide right here!'

The slugs held races, slow and steady,
While nearby squirrels were not quite ready.
One took a leap, and what a flop,
The crowd erupted, 'Don't you stop!'

The silence weighed, but not for long,
A voice emerged, a croaky song.
A cricket chirped, 'I lead the show!'
And every critter joined the row.

In quiet corners, smiles will sprout,
For even silence has its clout.
So come and join this funny scene,
Where moss and laughter reign supreme.

Guardians of the Canopy

The raccoons plotted, schemes so grand,
To steal some snacks from the kids' hand.
They donned a hat and shades for style,
And practiced sneaks with gleeful guile.

The owls exchanged their knowing looks,
'These kids can't outsmart our fun hooks!'
They hooted loud, a warning cry,
To keep the treats up oh so high.

The guardians watched the forest floor,
Where every prancing ant was sore.
As squirrels played tag amongst the trees,
With nimble tails, they danced with ease.

So join this crew of merry mischief,
Where fun's the rule, and laughter's riff.
In canopy's heart, the antics flow,
With every turn, the joy will grow.

The Parable of Spiraling Bark

Once a tree grew a funny twist,
Its bark like a spiraled, wavy mist.
Squirrels tried a flashy breakdance,
But ended up in a bumbling prance.

A rabbit laughed, with a cheeky grin,
As branches shook, where the antics begin.
The birds chirped tales of laughter loud,
While the owl sat perched, far too proud.

All in all, it was quite a show,
With laughter echoing high and low.
Nature's jesters, all on display,
In a bark-spun circus, come join the play!

Treasures of the Woodland Hideaway

In the woods where secrets gleam,
Lies a hideaway, a giggling dream.
Raccoons with masks, they hold a feast,
Eating snacks from a rainbowed beast.

A fox tells tales, with a twinkling eye,
Of treasure hunts that went awry.
He tripped on roots, fell with a thud,
And landed right in a puddle of mud!

Rabbits bounce near, with a joyful cheer,
While bees buzz tunes that only they hear.
In this woodland place, laughter is the key,
Unlocking joy as wild as the sea!

Whispers of the Canopy

High above, the leaves chuckle and sway,
As squirrels debate the best nut to play.
Chipmunks giggle at their own little fights,
Arguing over who spotted the lights.

A grand old tree in mossy attire,
Tells corny jokes that never tire.
The vines hang low, giving hugs to the ground,
While clumsy birds crash through, flapping around.

Hidden below, a snail takes a peek,
At gatherings where the forest critters speak.
With a smile so wide, it can't be denied,
The whispers above set off jubilant pride!

Secrets of the Silent Grove

In the silent grove, a secret unfolds,
Where mushrooms wear hats, and laughter bold.
A hedgehog plays tunes on a tiny flute,
While a dancing lizard jigs in a suit!

Beneath shady roots, an old tortoise sighs,
Telling tales of what bugs doing the fries.
"I saw a beetle with moves so fine,"
He chuckles, "He'd outdance any sign!"

Lights twinkle like stars in a vast blue sky,
As creatures gather 'round to give it a try.
For in this grove, where laughter's set free,
The secret of fun is the best kind of spree!

Reflections in Moss and Leaf

In shadows deep where squirrels play,
A leafy throne for those who sway.
They jest and chatter, nuts in tow,
Each acorn dropping, a tiny show.

The toad in green with eyes so wide,
Creates a splash, then takes a slide.
It's a comedy of hops and leaps,
Where nature laughs and seldom sleeps.

Frogs with crowns of lilypad wear,
Throwing banquets in the air.
With each plop and splash, they boast,
For bugs, they make the finest host!

And so we gather 'neath the twigs,
To share our tales and dance like pigs.
For here, amid the friendly cheer,
Life's silly moments draw us near.

The Ethereal Canopy

The leaves above are hats for trees,
Tickling branches in the breeze.
With whispers shared between the twirls,
They giggle softly, like the girls.

A wily woodpecker takes a crack,
At jokes that make the old bark crack.
The sunbeams peek with a bright grin,
As shadows dance like they're kin.

A squirrel jokes with a branch so long,
While owls sing a silly song.
And when the wind gives a light shove,
The laughter echoes, pure as love.

So here we bask, in nature's jest,
With every leaf our minds are blessed.
The canopy, a stage so bright,
Where humor dances, day and night.

Solitude in the Arbor

In quiet nooks where shadows dwell,
The trees spin yarns that weave so well.
A lazy cat naps on a branch,
While bugs on parade give a strange chance.

A lone chipmunk, with cheeks so round,
Shares secrets with mushrooms on the ground.
He chuckles softly, not a care,
In his hidey-hole, the world is rare.

The sun slips through, a playful light,
An audience for nature's sprite.
The branches sway a funny dance,
While all around, the critters prance.

In solitude, the laughter grows,
Where even thorns can bring some prose.
For in the stillness, joy is found,
Among the roots and hallowed ground.

Guardians of the Glade

A wise old tree with gnarled face,
Holds court for all in this fine place.
The beetles nod, the rabbits laugh,
Each small tale in the aftermath.

The owls, perched with watchful eyes,
Trade stories under the vast skies.
With flapping wings and beady stares,
They ponder life among the lairs.

A raccoon dressed in bold disguise,
Attempts to sneak under the skies.
But roots trip him, and down he goes,
In this glade, humor freely flows.

So here we stand, in nature's grace,
With woodland spirits in the chase.
Guardians of giggles, forever true,
In this wild haven, we laugh anew.

A Tangle of Dreams

A squirrel dreams big in a tree,
Of acorns and snacks, wild and free.
Yet slips on a twig, quite the scene,
Lands with a thud, where once he did preen.

The raccoons hold a meeting at night,
With masks and capes, oh what a sight!
They plan a heist on the bird feeder,
But end up snacking on their own sweeter.

A wise owl hoots, 'I need a break,'
From hooting and scouting, for goodness' sake!
He slips on his glasses, rests his head,
Dreams of the day when he's fed instead.

In the chaos of dusk, laughter resides,
As creatures below take delightful strides.
For in the wild, mishaps abound,
In every crack, joy can be found.

Moonlight Amidst the Foliage

The moon beams high, with a twinkling grin,
A firefly burst leaves the bats in a spin.
They fly in circles, doing the twist,
But crash into branches! Oh, how they missed!

A raccoon rolls over, claims he's a star,
In the stage lights of twinkling afar.
Yet stumbles on roots, with a comedic flair,
Falls like a pancake—a nighttime affair!

A chorus of frogs, in their muddy attire,
Croak out the tunes for the night to inspire.
In waltzing their way to a soft, sleepy tune,
The crickets join, as if hosting a swoon.

While shadows dance low, amid giggles and cheer,
In this woodland party, there's nothing to fear.
Nature's a jester, in this soft, silver sheen,
Where laughter and whimsy are fit for a queen.

The Secret Language of the Trees

The trees whisper secrets, intricate codes,
Of passing breezes and wandering roads.
A chipmunk listens, with ears perked high,
As leaves share tales of a bright blue sky.

But one oak got sassy, told jokes to the pines,
'Why don't we ever take the same lines?'
And all laughed so hard, they nearly did sway,
While branches stuck out in a fun, silly way.

A squirrel named Chester, with quite the flair,
Compares his nut stash to this and to that pair.
Yet the stash went missing in a gusty gust,
He'll moan about it, but first, he must rust!

Under the laughter, the forest feels bright,
Their quirks and their tickles amplify light.
For amidst the tall trunks lies humor so wise,
Nature giggles freely under sunny blue skies.

Portrait of the Woodland Spectrum

In colors so vivid, the forest awakes,
A palette of laughter, oh the fun it makes!
The yellows and greens, they swirl and they spin,
As butterflies sip on the nectar and grin.

With reds like the apples that dangle and tease,
The critters all rally, aiming to please.
As rabbits get dizzy in a hop, hop, hop,
They tumble right down, oh let the laughter pop!

The autumn leaves whisper, 'Join in the fun,'
As squirrels race past, eager to run.
Yet one little fellow forgot where to land,
And plopped in a puddle, mud-covered and bland.

So under the colors of this cool spectrum,
Mother Nature laughs, 'Oh, what a conundrum!'
With a tickle of light, and joyous esteem,
The woods come alive, all caught in the dream.

Shadows in the Thicket

Squirrels hold a conference, jokes at play,
While birds gossip secrets, chirping all day.
A wise old turtle laughs, in his slow-paced stride,
While rabbits reenact their favorite slide.

The bushes shake with giggles, rustling cheer,
As raccoons in masks bring a snack, oh dear!
A fox tries to dance, but slips on a root,
And ends up in a tangle, oh what a hoot!

Butterflies flutter, wagging tiny tails,
Singing off-key, like wind in the sails.
A hedgehog joins in, with a wobbly cheer,
Claiming he can spin like a whirling sphere.

Just another day, in this leafy nook,
Where laughter echoes wide, and smiles it took.
In the thicket's warmth, joy leaps and bounces,
With each little creature, silliness pounces!

Dance of the Leafy Abode

In a leafy place where shadows twirl,
A squirrel spins around, causing quite a whirl.
The leaves chime in, clapping with glee,
While a chipmunk tops the charts with his spree!

Frogs leap in time, their croaks a fine beat,
A turtle's slow shimmy can't be beat!
A chorus of crickets joins in the fun,
With rhythms and rhymes until day is done.

The moon peeks through, adding silver to sway,
While raccoons in bowties steal snacks—not play!
The owls hoot out wisdom, in laughter's refrain,
As the leafy abode spins, again and again!

Every creature recalls every jig and every shake,
In this joyous dance, no one's a mistake.
With a smile on their faces, they sway and they glide,
In this vibrant abode where fun cannot hide.

Echoes Among the Limbs

High up in branches, a parrot jokes loud,
As squirrels in caps form a giggly crowd.
Echos of laughter bounce off the trees,
Fluffy-tailed prancers move with great ease.

A crow joins the party, cawing a tune,
While beetles on branches make a dance floor soon.
A mischief of mice try their best to jive,
Creating a ruckus, they feel so alive!

A snail on a leaf coordinates the show,
With moves so slow that it's hard not to glow.
They twirl and they frolic in a colorful spree,
In this playful kingdom, where all come to flee.

As dusk blankets the fables of giggles incurred,
The night sings sweet dreams of laughter unheard.
Each echo among limbs holds joy's own sweet sound,
In harmony's arms, all funny things found!

Beneath Verdant Shadows

Where greenery shelters a jester's delight,
A raccoon in shorts gives a comedic fright.
With a waddle and wiggle, he issues a plea,
For the snacks of the day—where can they be?

A rabbit in tales tells of carrots galore,
But the punchline he drops leaves everyone sore!
As bad puns take flight, the canopies sway,
And laughter grows wild, brightening the day.

A woodpecker knocks out the rhythm of cheer,
While spiders in tutus swing with no fear.
In this shady retreat, every creature does play,
They turn silly dancing into art's own ballet!

With giggles aplenty, the stories unfold,
Of frolic and fun, and mischief untold.
So join in the joy, in this shadowy glade,
Where laughter is king, and silliness made!

Secrets of the Dappled Shade

In shadows where the squirrels play,
A cookie crumbles, come what may.
The sunbeams dance in joking flight,
While trees giggle, 'What a sight!'

The ants march in their tiny lines,
With secret tales of sugar finds.
A breeze sneaks in with playful cheer,
And whispers, 'Stay, there's fun right here!'

A picnic hat, a game of tags,
Where laughter leaps and joy just brags.
The leaves overhead snicker low,
While squirrels spill their acorn show.

So grab your snacks and bring a friend,
In dappled shade, the fun won't end.
With laughter ringing through the trees,
We'll find delight in every breeze.

The Embrace of Nature's Shadows

In shadowed realms where laughter reigns,
A critter dressed in silly chains.
With mischief dancing in the air,
Nature giggles, 'Come if you dare!'

A patch of grass, a wobbly chair,
Invisible friends giggle and stare.
A raccoon dons a quirky hat,
While rabbits argue, 'Is that my mat?'

The branches sway in jestful tease,
Tickling leaves with a gentle breeze.
And if you listen oh so close,
You'll hear the trees plot their next dose.

So find a nook and take a seat,
Let nature's whimsy be your treat.
For in the shadows, joy's within,
The funny side of life will win!

Serenade of the Branches

A warbler sings a silly tune,
While chipmunks tap their tiny spoons.
The sun throws sparkles, oh what glee,
As shadows waltz with lively spree!

A game of tag, the branches sway,
With giggles echoing in play.
The flowers blush in colors bright,
Joining in on this silly flight.

Oh, how the bushes sway and twine,
With whispers soft, 'You're doing fine!'
While mushrooms sport their polka dots,
And dance along with the wild tots.

So come and join this merry song,
In nature's arms, where we belong.
With every rustle, every cheer,
We find the fun that's always near.

A Refuge in the Thorns

Among the thorns, a jest unfolds,
With prickly jokes that nature holds.
A hedgehog chuckles as he rolls,
While thistles weave their funny goals.

The roses blush with a giggle flair,
As brambles join with fluffy hair.
A toucan splits a banana wide,
And shares the fruit on this wild ride.

In nooks and crannies, laughter pricks,
As flowers engage in wily tricks.
Each thorn a tale of humor told,
In this refuge, brave and bold.

So if you're lost, just take a chance,
In thorns and laughter, join the dance.
For in the wild, the fun abounds,
In nature's refuge, joy resounds!

The Hidden Haven

In a nook where squirrels play,
They hide acorns day by day.
A raccoon dances, quite a sight,
While the owl snoozes, what a fright!

Beneath the leaves, a party's grand,
With mushrooms laughing, hand in hand.
The fox cracks jokes, the deer take bets,
On who will forget where they left their pets!

The crickets chirp a comical tune,
While turtles waltz under the moon.
A hedgehog juggles with a pinecone,
In this spot that feels like home!

A rabbit wears a silly hat,
Chasing tales of a sneaky cat.
With all this fun, who needs a crown?
In this hidden spot, we wear our frown upside down!

Spirit of the Forest Floor

The mushrooms throw a wild rave,
While ants prepare a dance to save.
They twirl and spin, oh what a sight,
Caterpillar joins, igniting the night!

A critter spills some berry juice,
And suddenly everyone's let loose.
The groundhogs laugh, they can't believe,
How nature's floor is their reprieve!

A mole pops up to share a joke,
While sneaky rabbits try to poke.
Grasshoppers jump in gleeful cheer,
As fireflies blink, bringing good cheer.

All creatures sing, a funny tune,
Beneath the stars and shining moon.
In every corner, joy is found,
On this lively, giggling ground!

The Realm Under the Boughs

Under the arch of leafy green,
Laughter echoes, oh what a scene!
The stumps serve as a perfect chair,
For raccoons planning pranks with flair.

A friendly deer plays hide and seek,
While ferns sway and the creatures peek.
A chubby bear tries to fit in tight,
His belly aches, what a silly sight!

Squirrels trade tales, they're all aglow,
Of nuts that rolled and missed the show.
With every chuckle, the forest shakes,
In this realm where fun never breaks!

The sky shines through with a playful wink,
As bees buzz in tune, they start to link.
Joy thrives here, it's a comedy act,
In the woodland's embrace, we'll never lack!

Nature's Veiled Retreat

In the nook of twigs and leaves,
A chipmunk giggles, and then he weaves.
Through petals soft, he springs with glee,
Chasing his shadow, oh, let it be!

A wise old tortoise shares a tale,
Of slippery slopes and a wayward trail.
The frogs croak loudly, trying to sing,
While the spiders spin webs, a tangled fling!

Twilight descends with a sparkly glow,
As owl jokes about the bad show.
In this secret space, mischief brews,
And laughter echoes like morning dew!

With creatures here, the fun won't cease,
They share their antics, spreading peace.
In this hideaway, no frowns do meet,
It's Nature's retreat, where joy is sweet!

Echoes from the Grove

In the woods, a squirrel pranced,
With acorns thrown, he took a chance.
The trees laughed loud, a chuckle spree,
While birds joined in, oh what a glee!

A wise owl blinked with sleepy eyes,
'This party's wild, oh my, oh my!'
But just then, he lost his cool,
As a raccoon sneezed, he swooned like a fool!

The deer danced in their Sunday best,
While beavers hosted a nutty fest.
'This party's swell!' a rabbit sang,
As branches swayed, all a-twang!

So if you wander, hear the cheer,
In groves where laughter hangs so clear.
Just watch your snacks, they might disappear,
With critters ready to commandeer!

Under the Leaves' Embrace

Under the green, a picnic sprawled,
With ants in line, they proudly called.
A sandwich dropped, an eagle dove,
Oh what a mess, but watch them rove!

A fox arrived, with style and flair,
He wore a hat and a jaunty air.
The turtles groaned, 'Not this again!'
As he strutted past the woodland den.

The mice had cheese, a grand buffet,
Until the cats showed up to play.
They danced around, a comical sight,
In the leaf-shade, they laughed all night!

So come on down to this leafy spot,
Where every critter's a tricker and plot.
For when it's fun, all cares erase,
In the wilds' magical, quirky embrace!

The Sanctuary of Bark and Bloom

In the garden, bees buzzed with glee,
Spinning tales of honey and tea.
A gopher grinned, with soil on his snout,
'Let's throw a bash, there's no doubt!'

The daisies dressed up, flaunting bright hues,
While the clouds peeked down, not wanting to snooze.
A worm led the dance, wiggling wide,
While the daisies cheered from every side!

A chipmunk juggled berries galore,
As frogs croaked in rhythmic score.
'Watch your step!' cried a butterfly bold,
'You might end up in a story untold!'

With laughter and joy, the flowers did sway,
The sanctuary glowed at the end of the day.
With nature's antics, nothing to doom,
A party's alive in this bountiful bloom!

Murmurs Under the Foliage

A friendly chat among the weeds,
With ladybugs discussing their needs.
'Why does he think he's a garden king?'
A grasshopper chirped, jumping in spring!

The flower pots giggled, lips so merry,
While lizards played tag around a berry.
'Look at that snail, racing the clock!'
'Cheer him on, he's our backyard rock!'

The shadows danced, painted by light,
With critters twirling, oh what a sight!
Under the green, humor found its place,
As sunlight broke through, leaving no trace.

So if you wander where whispers play,
Join the fun in nature's array.
For in these leaves, laughter will roam,
Creating a bond, making you feel home.

www.ingramcontent.com/pod-product-compliance
Lightning Source LLC
Chambersburg PA
CBHW071839160426
43209CB00003B/351